R00311 66465

CHICAGO PUBLIC LIBRARY
HAROLD WASHINGTON LIBRARY CENTER

R0031166465

REF.
LB
2948
.S67   Ariyadasa, K. D.
A74
      Management of
         educational reforms
         in Sri Lanka

DATE		

cop. 1

FORM 125 M

The Chicago Public Library

APR 11 1979

Received

Experiments and innovations in education No. 25
An International Bureau of Education series

Management of educational reforms in Sri Lanka

by K. D. Ariyadasa
Deputy Director General of Education
(Curriculum Development and In-Service Education)
Ministry of Education, Sri Lanka

Study prepared
for the Asian Centre
of Educational Innovation
for Development

The Unesco Press-Paris 1976

The designation employed and the presentation of the
material in this publication do not imply the expression of
any opinion whatsoever on the part of the Unesco
Secretariat concerning the legal status of any country or
territory, or of its authorities, or concerning the delimitations
of the frontiers of any country or territory.

Published in 1976 by the Unesco Press
7, Place de Fontenoy, 75700 Paris, France
and the Asian Centre of Educational
Innovation for Development
Unesco Regional Office for Education in Asia
C.P.O. Box 1425, Bangkok, Thailand

English edition   ISBN 92-3-101372-6
French edition   ISBN 92-3-201372-x
Spanish edition   ISBN 92-3-301372-3

Printed in Singapore
by Singapore National Printers (Pte) Ltd.

© Unesco 1976 [B]

PREFACE

In 1972 Sri Lanka initiated a major reform of its education system. A series of six studies, of which the present publication is one,[1] describe the different aspects of education and how they were affected by the educational reform: in some aspects totally new programmes, designed and developed ground-up, were introduced; in others, the current programmes were reoriented, with new emphases and focal points.

The reform occurred in an education system which for quite a few decades had come to be taken for granted because of its steady rhythm of expansion and growth. As the present series of studies show, the driving force of the reform came from outside the education system, and lay in the urgencies of the social and economic situation. The changes triggered off in consequence within the education system are both comprehensive and fundamental, and serve to illustrate how the processes of reform and innovation are interlinked.

In order to ensure the successful implementation of the educational reform, particular attention was given to educational management. The basic thrusts in reorganizing the management process were: dialogue with the people, manpower development, and mobilization of available resources and technologies. Changes had to be made regarding the institutional infrastructure, administrative organization, staffing and allocation of functions.

The Secretariat, while noting that the views expressed by the author are not necessarily those of Unesco, records its appreciation to him for this valuable contribution to the series.

---

[1] The others are:
Ariyadasa, K.D. *In-service training of teachers in Sri Lanka.*
Premaratne, B. *Examination reforms in Sri Lanka.*
Peiris, K. *Integrated approach to curriculum development in primary education in Sri Lanka.*
Ranaweera, A.M. *Integrated science in the junior secondary school in Sri Lanka.*
Diyasena, W. *Pre-vocational education in Sri Lanka.*

REF
LB
2948
.S67
A74

cop.1
Soc

TABLE OF CONTENTS

		Page
1.	BACKGROUND	1
	1.1 *The Educational context*	1
	The period prior to 1971	1
	A brief overview of the educational reforms introduced in 1972	4
	1.2 *Identification of the problem*	7
	Inertia and stagnation	7
	The need to activate the management process	7
	The need to reform the management process	8
	1.3 *Origin*	9
2.	OBJECTIVES	11
	2.1 *A systems approach*	11
	2.2 *Dialogue with the people*	11
	2.3 *Manpower development*	12
	2.4 *Mobilization of resources and technologies*	13
3.	INSTITUTIONAL INFRASTRUCTURE	15
	3.1 *The organization before the reform*	15
	3.2 *Organizational changes*	16
	The creation of the post of Director (Planning)	16
	The new allocation of functions	16
	The creation of the Ceylon Education Service	19
	Trade union participation	19
	The organization of the Curriculum Development Centre	20
	3.3 *Organization and staffing*	21
	The Ministry	21
	The organization of the Ceylon Education Service	22
	Administrative and supporting service infrastructure	23

		Page
4.	HOW THE ORGANIZATION FUNCTIONS	25
	Planning	25
	Organizing (including staffing)	27
	Directing, including motivation	30
	Controlling	30
	Evaluation and feedback	31
	Informal channels	33
	Communicating	34
5.	PHASE OF REPLANNING	35
6.	RESOURCES	37
7.	CONSTRAINTS INHIBITING PROGRESS	39
8.	IN RESTROSPECT	41

1. BACKGROUND

1.1 The Educational context

The period prior to 1971

From what can be gleaned from recorded history, the management of education in Sri Lanka from the time of the institution of the Department of Public Instruction in the year 1869 has had a chequered past, no less chequered than the history of education itself with which it was inescapably interwoven. In the early years of the Department's existence, Her Majesty's Inspectors of Schools and other educators from Britain filled the berths of Directors of Public Instruction and Directors of Education. The concept of management of education had then hardly evolved, and efficiency in applying the rules of the codes of regulations in order to check over-payments of grants, salaries and wages was the criterion of efficient administration. The attitude towards management hardly changed even in more recent times. As late as the 1950s the hallmark of efficiency for an educational administrator was knowledge of the codes of regulations — there was a plethora of them — a Code for Assisted English Schools, a Code for Assisted Vernacular Schools and another for Government schools. Then there were the amendments to the regulations of the several codes passed by Parliament from time to time since the early twentieth century, the departmental circulars and, more important than these, there were the administrative precedents, that is, administrative fiats made on special occasions These were the things that mattered in the management of education.

The hallmark of efficiency for a field supervisor of education was his ability to detect malpractices committed by errant managers and heads of schools. The field supervisors were viewed, among other things, as the "eyes and ears" of the Department, and this expression epitomizes the duties they were called upon to perform and the roles in which they were cast.

This tradition of "efficient management of education" survived almost to the year 1960. Considering in retrospect the events of the last 30 years or more it appears as the enactment of two Acts of Parliament — The Assisted Schools and Training Colleges (Special Provisions) Act No. 5 of 1960 and The Assisted Schools and Training Colleges (Supplementary Provisions) Act No. 8 of 1961, and the consequent abolition of the system of assisted schools and the codes of regulations governing the payments of grants to assisted schools.

The changes that took place in educational management after all the assisted English and vernacular schools (barring a few which went private and unaided) were vested in the Government, should have been the occasion for introducing a truly national system of education and streamlining the management of the Department; but the opportunity went unheeded. No attempt was made to reorganize the content of education or to bring it into line with the hopes and aspirations of an independent and sovereign people. Perhaps the day-to-day problems resulting from the take-over of the assisted schools kept the Department fully occupied.

The legislation introduced in 1960 and 1961 left its impress on the management of the Department of Education. The Ministry had a problem on its hands. The codes of regulations were defunct. The managers of the assisted schools had been removed from the scene of activity and the Director of Education had assumed control of these schools. The Ministry's problem was the integration of the assisted schools with the Government schools and streamlining the management of the entire national educational system.

The Department of Education was up to this time highly centralized. A Director of Education and his deputies and assistants concentrated all power at the centre. The Director was assisted by nine sub-offices set up in the regions, but they were mere reporting outposts and little else. These nine sub-offices were headed by Education Officers. They had very little power to take decisions in education and even matters of little importance had to be referred to the Director of Education at the centre, sometimes even to the Permanent Secretary of the Ministry of Education. The orders handed down by the Permanent Secretary would go down the line via the Director of Education to the sub-offices for implementation. Any variations in these decisions had to be referred back up the line for decisions which again were handed back down the line for implementation. This system, apart from anything else, resulted in inordinate delay, and those who took decisions operated from an ivory tower to which others had no access.

The legislation enacted in 1960 and 1961 required changes in the administrative machinery of the Department. The term administration connotes a much narrower field than the term management. But this was initially not so, and the terms have been taken by some as being indistinguishable from each other. Even Fayol wrote "there is no one doctrine of administration for business and another for affairs of state; administrative doctrine is universal, principles and general rules which hold good for business hold good for the state too, and the reverse applies". So, when the Minister of Education directed, in 1961, that a conference of officers of the Department be hold to "explore the administrative set-up in the Department of Education with a view to making recommendations for any changes that may be necessary to gear administration to changed and changing conditions in the country", it was really the overhauling of the management of the Department of Education that he had in mind.

The conference, held in Bandarawela in April, 1961, made a signal contribution to the future management of the Department. The officers who met in Bandarawela were experienced men and women from all grades of the Department. The centralized approach to management, they recommended in their report, should be given up. And so it was. The number of regional outposts was increased to 23, of which 10 — the Educational Regions — were put in charge of Assistant Directors of Education, and 13 — the Educational Districts — were brought under Education Officers. Furthermore, the regions were given additional powers. Except for policy matters and certain other subjects that were reserved to the centre, other powers, including the disbursement of funds and establishment matters pertaining to the regions, were decentralized.

The process of decentralization was carried a step further in 1966. The decentralization of management in 1961 was considered a success. As the years went by, the education became the biggest state enterprise. Enrolments were increasing due to the growth in population and to increased participation. The enthusiasm for education unleashed by the recommendations of the Special Committee on Education in the mid-1940s which gave to Sri Lanka, inter alia, free education, was given a fresh impetus by the assumption of full state responsibility for education in the early 1960s. The expenditure on education was mounting and the situation called for a fresh look at the machinery of the Department that managed the school system.

The people had by now come into their own. In the mid-1950s, for the first time, they used the ballot to change the Government, and with this realization of the people's power, the representatives of the people realized that it was truly the people who were sovereign and not they. The need to consult the people and the teachers in all educational matters was also brought home to them.

In 1966, therefore, the decentralization of education was carried another step forward. On 1 October, 1966, the regional outposts were increased to 14 and they were given the status of full-fledged Departments of Government, and officers of the newly created rank of Directors of Education were appointed in charge of them. The districts were also upgraded and were put under the charge of Chief Education Officers. From time to time since then, the number of regions has been increased; they now number 18. The day that all powers are decentralized and the regions are made autonomous educational units, except for educational policy matters will see the final success of the decentralization programme recommended by the Bandarawela Conference. The Directors of Education, the Chief Education Officers and their staff are closer to the people than the officers at the centre and a two-way communication from the grass roots to the top and from the top down will then make the management process more realistic and meaningful.

Another important organizational change was effected in 1966 with the new decentralization of authority. The Ministry of Education and the Department of Education up to that time functioned as two discrete units. The Ministry was headed by the Minister of Education and a Parliamentary Secretary. It was staffed by a Permanent Secretary and an array of Assistant Secretaries. The Department was headed by a Director of Education assisted by an array of deputies and assistants. In 1966, with the establishment of Regional Departments of Education, the post of Director of Education was changed to the Director General of Education and was combined with the post of Permanent Secretary to the Ministry of Education. The two institutions, the Ministry of Education and the Department of Education, were amalgamated. This integration eliminated much duplication of work. Communication between the Ministry and the Department became direct and less cumbersome.

With the creation of the post of Director General of Education, which is only a statutory title carrying no extra remuneration, and its conferment on the Permanent Secretary of the Ministry of Education, three posts of Deputy Director General, each equal in status to the position of the head of a Class I government department, were created and were charged with the management of primary education, secondary education and technical education. So, when the present Government assumed power in 1970, the organization of the Ministry of Education at the top was as follows:

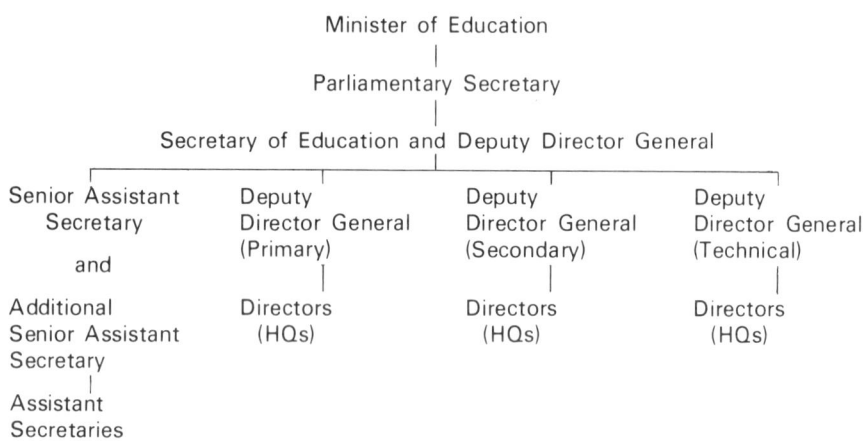

A brief overview of the educational reforms introduced in 1972

The reforms introduced in 1972 changed both the content and the structure of education. The structure was one of 5-3-4 (2 + 2) i.e. five years of primary, three years of junior secondary and four years of senior secondary education. The four years of senior secondary education were sub-divided again into two and two. At the end of the first two years, that is, after 10 years of schooling, pupils sat their first public examination for the award of the General Certificate of Education (Ordinary Level) based on which, some were selected for the next stage of education — senior secondary, which led to public examination for the award of the General Certificate of Education (Advanced Level). This also served as a university entrance examination. Both examinations, the G.C.E. (Ordinary Level) and the G.C.E. (Advanced Level) and the content of the courses were patterned very much on the British model.

This structure was changed to a 5-4-2-1 model. The five years of primary education were retained, the junior secondary stage was extended by one year making the open-access span one of nine years (5 + 4). The first public examination for the National Certificate of General Education was to be held at the end of the ninth year and it was based on the four year junior secondary course from grades VI to IX. On that basis, pupils were to be selected for the two-year senior secondary stage of education at the end of which, the Higher National Certificate of Education Examination was to be held. On that basis, pupils were to be selected for tertiary education. Those selected for university education would have the benefit of another year's education, intended to be the foundation year. This meant that the three years of rather aimless study in the junior school of the earlier system was changed to one of purposeful activity for four years leading to the National Certificate of General Education. It also meant a complete departure from the old model. Under the old dispensation specialisation began on entry to grade IX. The General Certificate of Education (Ordinary Level) course, starting in grade IX, streamed pupils into science, arts and commerce. In the more privileged schools, pupils were groomed for this specialization long before they reached grade IX. In effect, the open-access span ended with an examination held on the basis of specialized courses of study. There was, therefore, nothing basic about the course provided during the stage of basic education. In the new order there was no specialization in grades VI to IX. Every pupil had to follow a common curriculum consisting of 10 subjects, and had to present himself for all the subjects.

The content of education also underwent drastic change. The reforms were inspired by an earnest desire to democratize education. It was therefore decided to expose all the children in the junior secondary stage to an enriched common curriculum consisting of 10 subjects. Hitherto it was only the privileged schools that taught science and mathematics at the junior secondary level, and even with the introduction of mathematics for all in the junior secondary school in 1965 no attempt was made to provide qualified teachers to the schools that lacked them. The costs involved were probably taken as forbidding. But under the new reforms the common curriculum consisted, among other things, of English, science and mathematics and thousands of teachers were recruited in these subjects for service in the deprived schools.

The socio-economic needs of the country, the nature of the learners and the nature of knowledge were also given earnest consideration in the formulation of the new curricula. Grade IX was a terminal stage for large numbers of pupils. In addition there were also the dropouts who would not even reach grade IX. They had hardly figured in the educational thinking before. To add to this, only a small percentage of those who entered grade X would go through to the foundation year to tertiary education. These called for decisions on how to make education relevant to the needs of those who had to enter society without a secondary or a tertiary education. It was vital to give them an education of real value. Hence it was decided to make the marriage of the school and society real and effective. Some 80 vocations practised in the community at large were included in the curriculum for study. Schools had the freedom to select them in consultation with parents. A school had to select two or more vocations that lent themselves to 24 terms of study. Each had to be taught from grade VI to grade IX. Three terms a year in a four year course added up to 12 terms of work for each vocation. It was not only the practical skills that were to be inculcated; every attempt was made to invest the studies with an intellectual rigour that could well vie with the rigour that characterized the conventional disciplines.

In this attempt, community resources had to be harnessed at all stages — curriculum formulation, teaching, the in-service education of teachers and even in the assessment of pupil performance. In addition to these innovations, a process of curriculum renewal was also set in motion. Where knowledge was compartmentalized a unified or integrated approach was adopted. Social studies replaced history, civics and geography; Integrated science replaced physics, chemistry and biology and the new mathematics replaced the compartmentalized arithmetic, algebra and geometry. In general, the content of all subjects was updated.

In 1972 the reforms were introduced into the junior secondary school starting with grade VI — grade VI in 1972, grade VII in 1973 ending with grade IX in 1975. Beginning 1 January 1976, the senior secondary curriculum too is being changed to bring it into line with the reforms introduced into the junior secondary school in 1972.

At about the time the changes were introduced into grade VI, action was also initiated to consider the reforms that should be introduced into the primary school as well. The content of primary education was very much the compartmentalized traditional content that characterizes primary education in developing countries and this needed a thorough overhaul. The primary reforms were to be characterized by a new methodology altogether. A unified and integrated approach to curriculum formulation was adopted. Knowledge was, as far as practicable, to be built round certain themes and centres of interest drawn from the lives of pupils. Activity was to replace passivity. Informality and freedom would replace regimentation. The teacher was to structure the environment and guide the pupils and give up the authoritarian role he or she had played in the old scheme of things.

The same approach was taken in the junior secondary school. Knowledge based learning was to be replaced by knowledge based on activity and inquiry. Exploration of the environment, surveys and investigations, and the collection and analysis of data increasingly replaced the learning of facts doled out from textbooks. The old order was being completely transformed and the implications for the management of education were serious.

1.2 Identification of the problem

Inertia and stagnation

The education system had come a long way from what it was in the 19th and early 20th centuries. Brave attempts had been made to resurrect it and to make it serve the country's needs, for example the reforms ushered in the wake of the Special Committee Report in the mid-1940s and the legislation enacted in the 1960s leading to free education and to the taking over of assisted schools by the Government. But the enthusiasm generated by these had died down, and the education system, like the leviathan that it is, had sunk back into a state of inertia. The middle and the upper classes, in the main, reaped the plums in education and a few intelligent rural children also made the grade, thanks to free education and scholarships. The vast majority of the pupils, however, did not get an education that fitted them for life. They were being literally sacrificed for the sake of the few who sought admission to the institutions of higher learning. As time went by, even those who graduated through the school system and the universities found it increasingly difficult to find employment. The types of skills produced surpassed the absorptive capacity of the labour market. The education generated was, in the main, not of any use to society. As the ranks of the educated unemployed grew every year, the people lost interest in education, and the education system fell into a lethargy from which it was roused from time to time by various gimmicks that passed for the genuine thing. This lethargy, this inertia, affected the very core of the system and the Ministry could barely keep the wheels of the machinery of management on the move.

The need to activate the management process

The "revolt of the youth" that took place in 1971 gave a jolt to the system. This resulted in immediate stock-taking and planning for the future. It was decided to overhaul the education system with the following objectives in mind:
  (i) bring about a better 'fit' between the education system and the needs of the country at all levels of education;
  (ii) achieve greater internal quality and effectiveness within the system;

(iii) further the equality of access to education.

With these objectives in mind, the reforms sketched in earlier were undertaken. They have far-reaching implications for educational management. Phillip H. Coombs in his *The World Educational Crisis, a Systems Analysis*[1] indicates that a decision made to alter the education system's aims or priorities in some fashion — for example a decision to diversify secondary education, to include a new "technical" track to higher education, and new "terminal" programmes with a vocational bias — require far-reaching changes in the system's academic structure, in the curriculum and the teaching methods, in facilities and equipment and in the distribution of teachers and the flow of students within the structure. He concludes that, in short, every component is substantially affected by such a change.

It was evident to us that if the reforms we contemplated were to have a chance of success the whole management process had to be activated. The reforms were not thought of as altering "an education system's aims or priorities in some fashion", but as a thorough shake-up of the entire education system — its goals, aims and objectives, its content, methodology and structure. If the system was to deliver the goods the vital sub-systems had to function smoothly and effectively. A system that was ridden with inertia and lethargy had to be roused and infused with life and energy.

The need to reform the management process

There was, in fact, a need not only to make the sub-systems work but also to bring the management process as far as possible into line with scientific management concepts. Successful implementation depended largely on successful management. But, unfortunately, unlike in business or in industry, the scientific management of education has not yet been clearly formulated:

As enrolments, educational personnel, schools and expenditure continue to increase, the management of education becomes a task of formidable magnitude and complexity. Experience reveals that educational planning, as understood only a decade ago, is inadequate and that new approaches need to be developed. In most other respects — administrative structure, policy formation, operational procedures, research, information systems and evaluation — the elements of modern management are not yet available.[2]

Our situation was doubly difficult in that, we were not only confronted with the necessity to cope with the increases referred to in the World Bank statement but also with the necessity to reform the system's accepted values.

---

[1] Oxford University Press, New York, London, Toronto — 1968.
[2] Education, Sector Working Paper, World Bank — December, 1974.

1.3 Origin

It was in the middle of 1971 that the new reforms were discussed and planned. The decision that a beginning with the first year of the junior secondary school should be made from 1 January 1972, was also taken during these discussions. Immediately the machinery for the implementation of the reforms had to be considered. Even prior to the discussion of the new reforms, that is, as soon as the new Government came into power, some changes in the organizational set-up were, in fact, made; but serious thought to these problems was given only in about 1971. It cannot be said that the administrative set-up was completely changed. There was, as is explained elsewhere in this case study, an administrative infra-structure that could be used as a basis in the task of management, but, with a view to bringing the machinery of management into line with accepted management practises, to activating the process of management and to getting the system to shake off its lethargy, certain new structures had to be evolved and other changes effected.

All these took time and were worked into the system beginning in 1970. Once the objectives were established, and the plans developed and launched, feedback received from formal and informal sources made the Ministry decide on remedial courses of action. These courses of action included things as inconsequential to the whole system as the replacement of an uncommitted regional manager with one more committed, or as significant as deciding on a whole new campaign of briefing a category of officers not quite aware of their role in the new scheme of things.

The management of educational reforms was not carried out with one sweeping set of decisions taken at one point of time, but was spread over a long period of time beginning in 1970.

2. OBJECTIVES

2.1 A systems approach

Our all-pervading objective was, of course, efficient management. A systems approach to the problem offered the best prospects.

An education system, as a system obviously differs greatly from the human body — or from a department store — in what it does, how it does it and the reason why. Yet in common with all other productive undertakings, it has a set of inputs which are subject to a process designed to attain certain outputs, which are intended to satisfy the system's objectives. These form a dynamic, organic whole. And if one is to assess the health of an educational system in order to improve its performance and to plan its future its critical components must be examined in a unified vision.[1]

The relationship of the system's critical components was material to the efficient functioning of the system, and, as in the present case, when the reforms affected the vitals of the system, all of the critical components had a part to play in the implementation. Some, though, stood out as needing particular attention.

2.2 Dialogue with the people

Firstly, we had to enter into a dialogue with the people. This was a sine qua non for success. No educational system can function in a vacuum. It has its roots in the environment in which it functions. It draws its sustenance from it and, therefore, it is accountable to it.

A critical question in considering reforms is the scope and pace of change on the basis of a realistic assessment of the country's readiness. Awareness by the public of the need for change is the starting point for the development of a climate conducive to reform.[2]

With a history and a civilization dating back several millennia, society in Sri Lanka is tradition-bound. Traditions make people conservative. This imposes certain constraints on a reforming movement. Once the crisis was past, people might revert to their old values and their old ways of thinking, and, unless a dialogue was

---

[1] The World Educational Crisis. A Systems Analysis — Phillip H. Coombs.
[2] Education, Sector Working Paper, World Bank — December, 1974.

established, the reforms would have only a slender chance of success. The democratic egalitarian philosophy and the educational thinking that led to the reforms had to be made explicit to the people.

There was also the danger that dissidents and entrenched interests would turn obstructive. In democratizing education, in working for equity in education, new ideas like area quotas (we find this mentioned in the World Bank, Education Sector Working Paper) were mooted. We mooted this idea back in 1971. These would inevitably affect the chances of the most vociferous in society. Those who would gain from the reforms were the silent masses who hardly knew what was being mooted. Their support had to be enlisted.

2.3 Manpower development

The second pre-requisite for efficient management was manpower development. There were several aspects to manpower development. There was, firstly, the need to train efficient managers. They were required both at the top and in the middle grades. Without efficient management at the centre and at the periphery — the regions — the success of our plans would be very much in jeopardy. Then there was the need for the development of educational manpower. The changes in the curriculum required new skills, new knowledge, new thinking and new attitudes. The teacher force had to be given the necessary knowledge and skills and, more, their thinking and their attitudes had to be changed. Where necessary, additional teachers with the required new expertise had to be recruited. When it came to implementing the reforms it was necessary that both in management positions and in teaching positions there should be round pegs in round holes. If we failed in manpower development, staffing would provide considerable problems.

Inter-personal relationship was another aspect of this problem. In a vast network like the educational system of a country counting over one hundred thousand employees, distributed at several hierarchical levels, inter-personal relationships mattered very much. This is not easy to bring about. Nevertheless, strategies had to be evolved to recognize the contribution of each group and sub-group to the total endeavour, so that, they would work with one another in harmony and be motivated fully in achieving the goals, aims and objectives of the new programme.

On the teacher force depended much of the success of the new programme. If they were motivated the task would not present much difficulty. If they were not, whatever else was done would not count for much. Management by objectives brought to the fore the absolute necessity to motivate the teachers. Contact with the child was through the teacher and the child was our final objective. It was for him that we enriched the curriculum with the integrated science and the new maths. It was for him, in short, that we evolved a new curriculum. At this point, if we failed the reforms would fail. The teachers, therefore, mattered in a special way. The teachers had to be motivated and the relationship between them and the others in the system had to be carefully worked out.

2.4 Mobilization of resources and technologies

Thirdly, it was necessary to harness all the resources and the technologies available for the successful implementation of the reforms. Stock had to be taken of all the resources — human and material — and they had to be utilized to maximum advantage. Where resources were lacking, it was necessary to devise new technologies and methodologies to meet crisis situations. This applied to both manpower reserves and the software and hardware required for implementation.

These three then, viz: (a) entering into a dialogue with the people; (b) manpower development and the development of wholesome relationships among the ranks; and, (c) the mobilization of available resources and technologies were three important matters that stood out as requiring particular attention.

3. INSTITUTIONAL INFRASTRUCTURE

3.1 The organization before the reform

The organizational set-up that was in existence in 1970 was referred to briefly earlier on. There was the Permanent Secretary[1] to the Ministry of Education who was also the Director General of Education. Three Deputy Directors General of Education, one in charge of primary education, one in charge of secondary education and the other in charge of technical education functioned under him. The picture must now be completed by setting out the vital sub-systems of the education system.

Three of the important units were those that dealt with school works, school supplies and land acquisitions. The first which was headed by the Director of School Works, a qualified engineer, came under the Permanent Secretary. The second, which came under the Chief Accountant of the Ministry and the third which came under an Assistant Secretary were supervised by the Permanent Secretary through his senior Assistant Secretary.

Teacher education which was headed by a Director of Education functioned under the Deputy Director General of Primary Education and, after the reallocation of functions, under the Deputy Director General (Schools Organization).

There was another important unit in charge of the appointment and the deployment of teachers. This was the Schools Administration Unit which was headed by a Director of Education. This too came under the Permanent Secretary himself and, he supervised it through his Senior Assistant Secretary. The unit that was in charge of the administration of the Ceylon Education Service was headed by an Assistant Secretary and this too came under the Permanent Secretary who supervised it through his Senior Assistant Secretary.

The fact that the Schools Administration Unit, the Supplies Unit, the School Works Unit and the Land Acquisition Unit came under the Permanent Secretary who worked some of them through the Senior Assistant Secretary, did not amount to their being separated from the activities of the Deputy Directors General. In all matters pertaining to their work the Permanent Secretary, acting as Director General, consulted his three deputies. The set-up is as indicated in Chart I.

---

[1] Under the new Constitution the Permanent Secretary is designated Secretary, Ministry of Education.

The regional set-up is as described in Section 1.1. The organization of a Regional Department of Education is as indicated in Chart II.

In a region the Department of Education was headed by the Director of Education, assisted by a number of Chief Education Officers and Education Officers. It also had its office organization with an Administrative Officer from the combined Administrative Service, an Office Assistant, an Accountant from the Accountants' Service, a Financial Assistant and supporting staff to assist him in the management of the schools. An education district had a District Office headed by a Chief Education Officer and supporting staff. A District Office differed from a Regional Office in that it had no payments division. All payments in the districts were made by the Regional Departments of Education with which they were affiliated.

The region and the districts were territorially sub-divided into Education Circuits which were in charge of Circuit Education Officers. In the field, in addition to the Circuit Education Officers there were Specialist Education Officers appointed on a subject basis, as for instance, a Specialist Education Officer in Science and a Specialist Education Officer in English to assist the Directors of Education and the Chief Education Officers in the supervision of the educational programme.

3.2 Organizational changes

The creation of the post of Director (Planning)

One of the important new changes that was brought into being by the new Government was the creation of a post of Director of Planning which was subsequently elevated to the position of Deputy Director General (Planning). This was an essential pre-requisite to successful management. The creation of a new division for educational planning not only took note of the necessity for planning in management, but also institutionalized all those processes and activities that go with planning and made it the responsibility of an important division in the Ministry. This did not create the cleavages that sometimes characterize the staff-and-line relationships in industry. Planning in education cannot be done in isolation and all senior officers have to get together in the planning of the activities of the Ministry. It, however, helped organize the process of planning which hitherto lacked an institutional framework.

The new allocation of functions

Along with the creation of the post of Deputy Director General (Planning) the functions of the three Deputy Directors General were reallocated. Instead of the division into primary, secondary and technical education the new allocation of functions were (a) educational planning, (b) educational design, in-service education of teachers and research, and (c) schools organization and implementation. This was

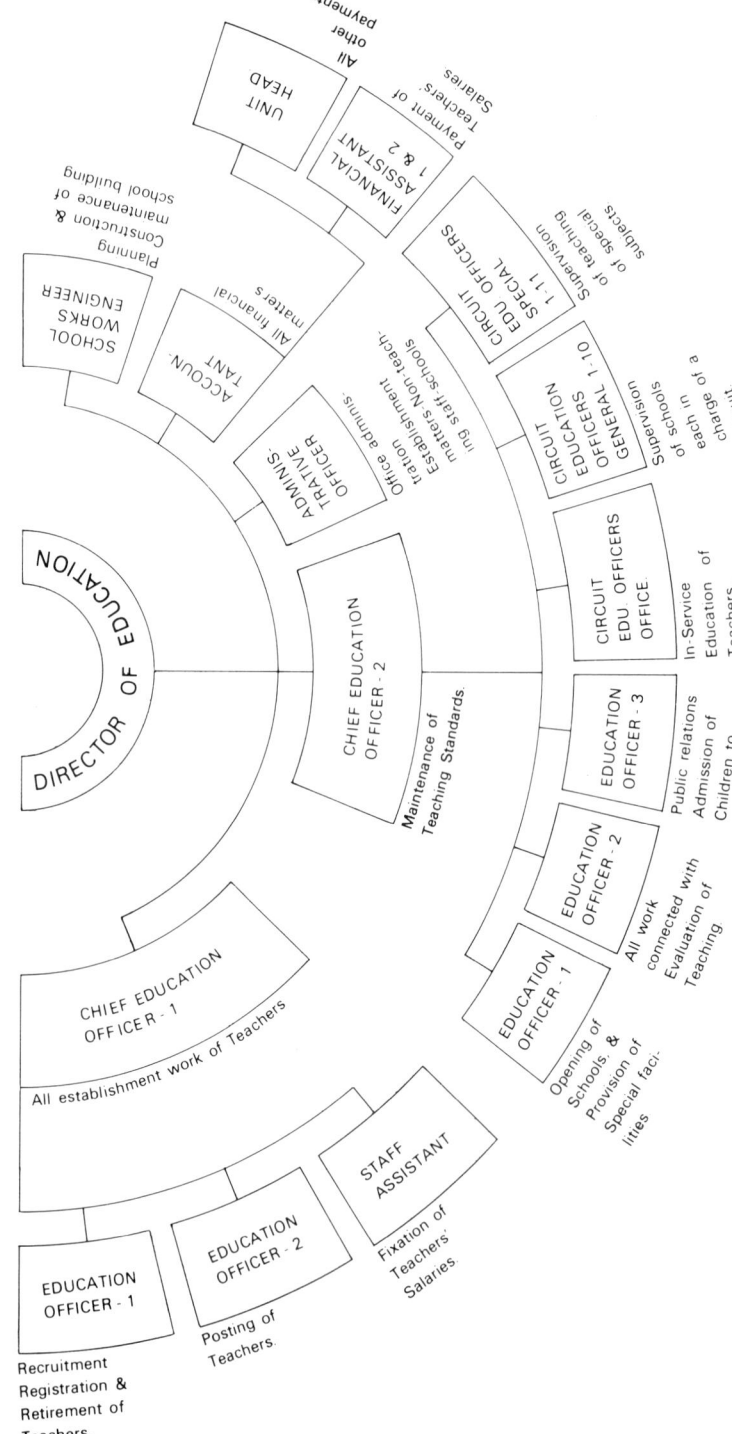

CHART II

ORGANIZATIONAL CHART OF COLOMBO SOUTH EDUCATION REGION

a much more workable arrangement since it cut across the barriers of functions. This allowed a unitary approach to education and permitted the three Deputy Directors General to come together with the Director General for discussions in all matters affecting the entire school system.

The creation of the Ceylon Education Service

Another important step was the creation of the Ceylon Education Service, on 15 October 1971, by the publication of "The Minutes on the Ceylon Education Service" in the *Ceylon Government Gazette Extraordinary* (No. 14, 979/8) of 12 October 1971. It created an Education Service comprising five classes which were sub-divided into the general cadre and the special cadre. The special cadre was provided to cater to special subject needs. Since the inception of the education service there has been a constant interchange among the ranks of Directors of Education, Chief Education Officers, Education Officers and Circuit Education Officers on the one hand and the corresponding grades of principals of schools on the other.

Management has been defined as a social process in which one constantly makes use of other people in achieving goals. If the goals are to be achieved through other people, it becomes necessary to motivate them to greater effort in the achievement of these goals. One kind of motivation is intrinsic. This was stimulated by helping teachers to see real value in the changes initiated.

Through the creation of the Ceylon Education Service the top rungs of management were open to a much larger clientele. Any qualified teacher who showed qualities of leadership could aspire to being a head of a school. It was much easier to become a head of a school than to enter the administrative hierarchy, but under the new dispensation, being a head of a school conferred the same status as being in that hierarchy. To those who could not be heads of schools, the opportunity was open to enter the service at the Class V level and to serve in a wide range of positions. The important thing is that those who belonged to what has sometimes been referred to as the educational proletariat were now given a place in the management of affairs.

Trade union participation

Another very important change that was written into the structure of the Ministry was the recognition extended to trade unions, not only of teachers, but of all categories of employees in the Ministry. With this recognition the trade unions of teachers, the trade unions of the clerical staff and the trade unions of other categories of employees became very active. In fact, it has extended beyond mere recognition and permitted active participation in some areas of management.

Councils of trade unions have been formed to advise the Secretary on how to cut waste, conserve resources and maximize output.

Even when the annual programmes of work are drawn up, the trade unions are consulted. Representatives of trade unions sit on teacher transfer boards and generally participate in all activities of the Ministry. This is a healthy sign that needs to be fostered with a view to giving all ranks of employees a sense of belonging to the Ministry.

The organization of the Curriculum Development Centre

By 1970, the Curriculum Development Centre had come into being, but did not quite enter into the life of the Ministry. Administratively it came under the Deputy Director General, (Secondary Education) and was pre-occupied mainly with science and mathematics education. The reforms initiated in 1972, the management of which is the subject of this case study, were in the main curricular reforms and the Curriculum Development Centre had to play a large part in implementing them. This was foreseen at the very inception and the new organization of work made curriculum development and the in-service education of teachers the duties of one of the three Deputy Directors General. Moreover, the Centre staff was expanded to cope with its new responsibility in the matter of formulating the new curricula and in carrying out connected research, studies and the in-service education of teachers at all levels. The Centre expanded, virtually, to the size of a new department. The staff of the Curriculum Development Centre was increased to include the following:

Deputy Director General	... 1
Directors Grade II	... 3[1]
Chief Education Officers	... 3
Education Officers	... 12
Other staff (clerks, stenographers, typists and other ancillary grades)	... 59
Teachers, Teacher Educators and other professional staff	... 100[2]

In keeping with its new role, the Curriculum Development Centre has also been given its own identity in the *Estimates of Expenditure* of the Government. The programme of activities of the Centre and the finances voted for the current year are as follows:

(These are funds voted for the various activities only, and do not include the salary component and other items of recurrent expenditure)

---

[1] There are now 5 Directors of Education.
[2] Government Estimates — 1975.

Head 48 — Ministry of Education
Programme 2: General Education
Project 1: Design, In-service Education and Research

08 Other Services

1.	In-service Training	Rs. 1,500,000
2.	Evaluation, Other Studies and Research	Rs. 203,000
3.	Syllabus, Courses and Textbooks	Rs. 350,000
4.	Population Education	Rs. 1,006,000 *
		Rs. 3,059,000

* UNFPA Aid Rs. 807,000. This includes the salary component of the staff of the Population Education Project.

The Ministry of Education has two other Departments which play vital parts in the management of educational reforms. They are the Examination Department and the Department of Educational Publications. The Commissioner and certain categories of officers serving in these two Departments are also included in the Ceylon Education Service.

3.3 Organization and staffing

The Ministry

It will be clear by now that the Ministry was being organized on a new functional footing. The new division of activities — planning, design (curriculum development), in-service education and research, and school organization and implementation are, as we have observed earlier, a much more practical orchestration of functions.

Then there are the maintenance sub-systems. The pre-service education of teachers is better viewed as a maintenance sub-system than as an adaptive subsystem, especially in reference to the implementation of reforms. Educational design which connotes, in the main, the development of new curricula, the in-service education of teachers and research and studies in the context of reform, have to be considered as forming an adaptive function; and the Curriculum Development Centre has, therefore, to be considered as an adaptive sub-system. The planning function has to be viewed as a managerial function and the Planning Division as a managerial sub-system. The Organization and Implementation Division is both a managerial and a maintenance sub-system.

The School Administration Unit which has a vital maintenance function to perform is a key unit of the Ministry, in that it is in charge of the recruitment and the deployment of teachers. Three other key maintenance sub-systems are the Supplies Unit, the School Works Unit and the Land Acquisitions Unit. These were critical sub-systems in implementing the reforms and they worked as a closely knit complex.

The Department of Examinations and the Department of Educational Publications were headed by Commissioners — one was designated the Commissioner of Examinations, the other the Commissioner of Educational Publications. The Commissioner of Publications performed a maintenance function. He was, for the most part, responsible for the production and distribution of school textbooks. The Commissioner of Examinations was responsible for conducting the examinations that replaced the General Certificate of Education (Ordinary Level) and the General Certificate of Education (Advanced Level). Both Commissioners came under the Secretary to the Ministry of Education.

The organization of the Ceylon Education Service

Reference has already been made to the creation of the Ceylon Education Service. The *Minutes on the Ceylon Education Service* which brought the Service into being with effect from 15 October 1971, created 12 posts in Class I and 35 posts in Class II. Classes III, IV and V were sub-divided into general cadre posts and special cadre posts. In Class III, provision was made for 42 general cadre and 44 special cadre posts; in Class IV for 20 general cadre and 71 special cadre posts; and in Class V for 662 general cadre and 158 special cadre posts. These numbers have been increased from time to time considering the requirements of the Service.

The posts of Commissioner of Educational Publications and Commissioner of Examinations are included in Class I of the Education Service. Directors of Education of the larger regions and Directors in certain other key positions of the Ministry are also included in Class I. The majority of the Directors of the regions and the Directors of the Ministry and certain grades of officers in the Departments of Educational Publications and the Department of Examinations are included in Class II. Class III officers normally serve as Heads of District Education Officers. They also assist the Regional Directors in Regional Departments of Education and serve in the Ministry and the Departments of Educational Publications and Examinations. Class IV officers also serve in the Ministry, in the Regional Departments of Education, the District Offices and the two Departments of Educational Publications and Examinations. Class V officers function mainly in the Education Circuits and are designated Circuit Education Officers. Officers of all these classes function as principals of schools. This, in effect, means that an officer of a class in the Ceylon Education Service who is functioning as a principal of a school may be interchanged with an officer of the same class who is working in the Ministry, a region or a department. On many occasions principals have exchanged places with Directors of Education.

In the scheme of recruitment for the respective classes the following stipulation has been included:

Should after 1.1. 1975 have a minimum of two years' experience as a teacher or lecturer or Principal of a school. This experience should be within the six years immediately preceding the date on which applications close.

This in effect requires all officers of the Ceylon Education Service to have after 1 January 1975 a minimum of two years' teaching experience, within the six years immediately preceding, for promotion to the higher classes of the service.

Administrative and supporting service infrastructure

Some of the other services that participate in the management of education are the Combined Administrative Service, the Accountants' Service and the Government Clerical Service. The Combined Administrative Service, which replaced the old Colonial Civil Service, is concerned with the management of education in a big way. The Senior Assistant Secretary and the Assistant Secretaries of the Ministry of Education and the administrative officers of the Regional Departments of Education are drawn from this Service.

The Chief Accountant and the Accountants both in the Ministry and the Regional Departments of Education belong to the Accountants' Service, and they assist the Secretary, who is the Chief Accounting Officer of the Ministry and the Heads of the Regional Departments of Education in the management of educational finances.

4. HOW THE ORGANIZATION FUNCTIONS

Planning

"The basic management function is planning, which begins with setting objectives and includes specifying the steps needed to reach them". To follow such a textbook definition in outlining the process of planning or, rather, re-planning the education system would be futile. The need for a full-scale reform of the education system had been felt for a long time. The Government that assumed power in May 1970 immediately addressed itself to the task. The Government that was replaced had also attempted to reform the education system and, in fact, a Bill to that effect had been tabled in Parliament. This Bill died a natural death due to differences of opinion and was never taken up for debate.

Immediately after the new Government assumed power, top-level discussions took place on the nature of the education reforms that should be introduced. The intention was to draft another bill, but political events made that untimely. The "revolt of the youth" in early 1971 rocked the country. The Government itself came out with important new legislation for the social amelioration of the people. The Ministry of Education, too, sensed that the time was opportune for replanning education.

A Division for Educational Planning was set up with a Director of Planning in charge. A further series of high-level conferences, some of which were chaired by the Minister in person, followed and it was agreed that everything possible within the framework of existing legislation should be done to overhaul the education system.

The conferences that were convened with the Secretary and Director General presiding, comprised teachers, trade union representatives, Ministry officials and university dons. The discussions were free and frank. The current situation was examined and the problems arising therefrom were analysed. Objectives were mooted and, against the background of these objectives, all possible alternative approaches were considered. The requirements of resources, both human and material, were assessed. Cost-benefit considerations were discussed. Organizational and implementational aspects were considered. Finally, a plan of action for the five-year period 1972 to 1976 was designed and issued in 1971, as a preliminary draft. This was subsequently revised and issued as the *Medium Term Plan for the Development of Education 1972/76*.

It is appropriate at this point to quote from the foreword written by the Minister to the *Medium Term Plan for the Development of Education 1973/77*, as it places the proposals for education in the context of overall planning and outlines the function of planning in the management of educational reforms.

"The five year plan of the Sirimavo Bandaranaike Government (1972-76) which was presented in November, 1971, diagnoses the limitations of the education sector in the following terms:

The basic shortcoming of the country's education system is that the academic type of curricula are framed to cater to the needs of that small minority of the output of the educational system who having reached the G.C.E. (O.L) compete for the very small number of jobs available as doctors, engineers, administrators or teachers. Of the others, a small number obtain employment in the clerical, technical and service occupations, while the rest begin the interminable wait for the white-collar jobs that are not there. Judging from the results it is no exaggeration to say that the social returns to educational investment have been negligible, if not negative.

The failure, if not the inability, of the academic system to provide a meaningful and a productive role for the output of the educational system has resulted in fear, frustration and despair rather than a net increase in social satisfaction. Thus it becomes evident that an educated population becomes a national asset only to the extent that it is able to fit into the productive occupations that the economy is capable of providing.

Based on this diagnosis, the Government's five year plan of development spells out the objectives and the strategy for educational development in the years ahead:

The main objective of the curricular change that is to be inaugurated from 1972 is to integrate the academic and vocational aspects of education in the general school system. It seeks to equip students with a good general education together with a basic familiarity with one or more vocational opportunities available to them. This does not mean any reduction in academic content.

What it means is that the materials taught and the whole idiom of teaching has meaning for the student and will stand him in good stead when he leaves the system.

In pursuing this policy, the Ministry of Education formulated a five-year programme of development, 1972-76, in close collaboration with the Ministry of Planning and Employment. Its proposals were approved by the Government in August 1971 and were implemented, commencing with grade VI, in 1972. It is significant to note that these development proposals were discussed with groups such as teachers, professional educationists and trade union organizations with a view to obtaining their whole-hearted support in implementation.

Having prepared the medium-term plan, the Planning Division in consultation with the project staffs next reduced it to a series of annual plans which specified the targets for each sub-system of the education system. These annual plans provide the basis for programming.

The work that has devolved on the Planning Division of the Ministry can be summarized as follows:
- (a) Preparation of the medium-term plan.
- (b) Preparation of implementation programmes.
- (c) Assisting in the preparation of the programme and performance budget.
- (d) Reviewing progress through the maintenance of the operations room.
- (e) Conducting the annual school census and the maintenance of a management information system.
- (f) Man power development in the area of educational management.

The Planning Division of the Ministry is still in its infancy, having been established in 1971. The Deputy Director General (Planning) keeps constantly in communication with the other Deputy Directors General, the heads of units and with the Directors of Education of the regions and the heads of departments; and horizontal communication (throwing "gangplanks", as it were) helps a great deal in these activities. Lines of communication in the Ministry permit the various divisions and units to communicate with one another. Besides, all important activities and issues are discussed with the Secretary, the three Deputy Directors General, the other senior officers like the Commissioner of Examinations and the Commissioner of Educational Publications and the heads of other units coming together.

Organizing (including staffing)

The decentralization of the administration of the Ministry carried out in 1961 and again in 1966 had given the Ministry an organizational infrastructure. If this set-up could have been taken to its logical conclusion, and if every revenue district could have been given a Regional Department of Education that would have served our purpose better. But this could not be done because of resource constraints. The number of regional offices was, therefore, increased gradually.

The significant and far-reaching changes effected in the organizational set-up of the Ministry were referred to in paragraph 3.2. They will be repeated only when the present discussion requires it.

The division of work at the centre had been put on a functionally rational basis. A set-up in which one Deputy Director General was in charge of planning, another in charge of design (i.e. curriculum), in-service education and research, and a third in charge of school organization and implementation was rightly tailored to efficient organization. The earlier division into primary, secondary and technical education resulted in compartmentalization and a duplication of functions which hindered rather than helped the management process.

The objectives of each division were clearly defined and so was accountability. The classical theory of management requires that when a man is held responsible for attaining certain objectives he should be given the necessary authority to achieve those objectives. In actual practice, in a complex institution such as a Ministry of Education, this is sometimes not possible. Take, for example, the Curriculum Development Centre which was charged with the responsibility of developing the new curricula and training the new manpower required to teach them. Fair numbers of the right kind of people with the right kind of expertise in subjects such science and mathematics were required for this work, and they had to be obtained from the school system. Since there was a dearth of teachers in the sciences and mathematics, it was not always possible to demand and obtain their release. These were some of the constraints under which the staffing function had to be carried out.

The co-ordination of work among the various divisions of the Ministry was ensured by regular meetings of the heads of divisions. The co-ordination between the Ministry and the regions was similarly ensured by regular meetings with Regional Directors of Education and the Chief Education Officers of the districts. Recently, the regions have been zoned and three Deputy Directors General have been put in charge of these zones in addition to their work. This has resulted in closer contact between the Deputy Directors General and the regions. Regular discussions are held and through the circulation of the minutes of such discussions a measure of co-ordination between the Ministry and the regions is maintained.

Co-ordination within divisions or units is the responsibility of the head of the division or unit who is invariably a Deputy Director General, Director, Chief Accountant, Assistant Secretary, Accountant or Chief Education Officer. Methods and procedures relating to the internal workings of divisions or units are well established and regulated. A unit on "organization and method" assists other units in maintaining organizational efficiency.

Staffing is a critical component of the process of organization. It is done on the basis of the responsibility and the volume of work devolving on each division. Stock is taken from time to time and the cadres are revised.

An important aspect of staffing is manpower development. The necessity to develop managerial skills led to several seminars and training programmes. Some of these were conducted jointly by the Ministry of Education and the Administration and Planning Division of the Unesco Regional Office for Education in Asia, Bangkok. The Sri Lanka Academy of Administrative Studies also takes part in training top-level managers in education. Recourse is also had to programmes conducted by the I.I.E.P., International Institute of Educational Planning, Paris. This function of organizing the training of top and middle-level managers in education devolves on the Planning Division of the Ministry of Education.

The development of the manpower necessary to implement the new curricula was entrusted to the Curriculum Development Centre, which, with a country-wide programme of in-service education of teachers, has up to now discharged that responsibility.

This programme entitled the In-service Training of Teachers in Sri Lanka was case studied for the Unesco Regional Office for Education in Asia, Bangkok, and will therefore not be dealt with in detail here.

The mobilization of all the resources available was clearly required for the success of the reforms and this was part of the organizational effort. The various strategies used to harness the human resources have been described elsewhere in this paper. The software and hardware required posed problems of mammoth proportions.

Since equipment was in short supply, the Science Curriculum Committee had to muster all its ingenuity and expertise to tailor the curriculum to reality and yet make it a worthwhile programme. Much dead wood had to be removed from the earlier curriculum and the result has been favourably received in science circles. Lavish laboratories could not be afforded any longer. Instead we had now to provide science rooms to thousands of schools. This required changes in the blueprints. Paper and printing also posed problems. Every effort was made to economize and to use resources to the best advantage. Conferences had to be called regularly and when one institution could not perform a function by a due date, another institution was called upon to step in to fill the breach.

So it was with human resources. When there was a short supply of graduates from the 12-year school to fill the berths of teachers of science and mathematics, graduates from the 10-year school were recruited. But this in turn required an intensification of the in-service education programme to bring them up to scratch. It was also envisaged that with the new reforms the numbers who would seek admission to the science and mathematics courses in the senior secondary school would increase sharply. This would require additional supplies of science and mathematics graduates as teachers. To supply them would take time and, therefore, to prepare teachers for science and mathematics, the University of Sri Lanka instituted the Diploma in Science and the Diploma in Mathematics for would-be teachers of science and mathematics at the senior secondary level. Those who passed these courses would swell the ranks of the graduates who passed the regular graduate courses each year.

In the organizational set-up, it must be admitted, the teacher colleges have not been in the forefront in the implementation of reforms. This was mainly because teacher colleges impart regular basic training that prepares uninitiated teachers to an awareness of their professional roles. But the reforms could not wait, and the teacher colleges catered only to a fraction of the teacher force involved in the implementation of the reforms. The teacher colleges have now fallen in line with the new reforms and their curricula reflect the changes that have taken place in the school system.

Directing, including motivation

A discussion of what is good management and what provides motivation is only of academic interest. Suffice it to say that, initiative, drive and quality of leadership play an important part in good management. These qualities are carefully considered in selecting those who are to direct. Technical competence gives these directors confidence to lead. To acquire this in the field of procedure, they are required to attain a thorough grasp of all the rules and regulations pertaining to their jobs. The *Minutes of the Ceylon Education Service* prescribe that the first efficiency bar for officers in the service will consist of an examination in:

(1) Public Commission rules[1] and government regulations;
(2) Accounts;
(3) Education law; administration and supervision; and
(4) Second language.

The second language is Sinhala for Tamil officers and Tamil for Sinhala officers.

To complete the second efficiency bar the officers are required to obtain professional or post-graduate qualifications in education.

The minimum basic qualifications required for admission to the various classes of the Ceylon Education Service are high. These ensure that those selected will be equipped with a basic minimum of procedural and technical expertise to do their jobs. Other qualities are considered at the time of selection.

Motivation is essential for successful direction. This was built into the system at all levels from the very beginning. The top echelons of the service, which had been open only to a coterie of officers, were thrown open to the rank and file of the service. Principals and teachers were admitted in large numbers to the various classes of the Ceylon Education Service. This has given the rank and file — the educational proletariat, as it were — a sense of participative management in the affairs of the Ministry. The inter-changeability of heads of schools with Chief Education Officers and Directors of Education has also given the Ministry a wider catchment area from which to select top-and middle-grade managers. Then again, the recognition extended to the trade unions in matters affecting them, such as their own transfers, and in the overall management process, such as in budgetting, has given them also a sense of participative management. These have helped the direction of educational affairs at all levels.

Controlling

In the terminology of management, controlling is the process by which managers appraise progress in terms of the plans, and this is done on the basis of feedback and evaluation. In a system such as the education system of a country, this

---

[1] This was under the old Constitution. It has been replaced under the new Constitution with *The Manual of Procedure.*

is a very difficult and complex problem. Firstly, there is the overall plan. Secondly, every sub-system has its own plans geared to the overall plan. Therefore, in controlling, it becomes necessary for every sub-system to take stock of its performance against its own and for the entire system to take stock of the performance of all sub-systems against the overall plan of action. This requires the co-ordination of all plans. If one system lags behind the whole plan will suffer.

Let us take a few examples. The Curriculum Development Centre was charged with providing the new curricula and new textbooks and with training the teachers in service for successful implementation. The Centre had to set up its subject committees and the work of the subject committees had to be co-ordinated. The curriculum material and the textbooks had to be made available by a given date, fixed in consultation with the Schools Organization Division and the Department of Educational Publications. The work of printing the curriculum material and textbooks and distributing them was done by these organizations, and it entailed very complicated procedures. Therefore, control had to be exercised in planning the work and it was necessary to keep meticulously to the plans. This made it necessary to adopt rather sophisticated procedures like programme evaluation and review techniques. What made this operation all the more delicate was that quality control required that so many experts participate in the planning, the development and the evaluation and revision of these materials. The writing of instructional material could have gone on for years depending on the time available for trial and revision, but the work had to be tailored to a tight schedule. The in-service education of teachers had also to be planned and phased so that the training synchronized with the implementation of the curricula in the schools.

The Schools Organization Division had to control its activities so that the printing and distribution of the instructional material took place on time, and the necessary equipment and supplies reached the schools on time. Then there was the matter of teacher recruitment. Thousands of science, mathematics and English teachers were recruited and their appointment and deployment had to be synchronized with the other activities. Each sub-system had to have its own plans and performance had to be measured against these plans. These had to be co-ordinated and the overall performance had to be checked. The latter function was carried out by the Planning Division which set up an operations room for the purpose.

Evaluation and feedback

To check progress against plans, feedback and evaluation are necessary. Management by objective requires that the main objectives should be kept constantly in mind. Some of the targets could be physically checked, e.g., whether or not the books, equipment and teachers had reached the schools on time. If there were any shortfalls they could be checked and action taken to remedy matters. But the intangibles in education, e.g. the quality of the instructional system, could not be measured. Therefore to check both the tangibles and intangibles, diverse types of feedback had to be obtained.

This feedback was received through both formal and informal channels. The feedback obtained through formal channels took the following forms:
  (a) feedback from conferences of Circuit Education Officers;
  (b) feedback from conferences of Regional Directors of Education and Chief Education Officers in charge of districts;
  (c) feedback from conferences with Deputy Directors General of Education;
  (d) feedback from teams and committees visiting schools;
  (e) feedback obtained at Ministry and Treasury conferences to check progress against the targets set in the programmed and performance budget;
  (f) feedback from evaluation of student performance and other types of surveys;
  (g) feedback from school inspections.

Conferences of Circuit Education Officers are a regular feature. They are held mostly at the regional level with the Regional Directors of Education and Chief Education Officers in charge of districts presiding. Sometimes the Director General and his deputies also attend. At these meetings valuable information on how the plans are progressing is obtained. Shortcomings are highlighted and, on the basis of these discussions, remedial action is taken. At times, re-planning takes place. The Curriculum Development Centre brings the Circuit Education Officers regularly to the Centre both to brief them on the centre programmes and activities and to obtain information on how the Centre programmes are being carried out.

At conferences of Regional Directors of Education valuable information in respect of the regions is obtained. These have been a regular feature. Of late, the island has been divided into three zones and each zone has been brought under a Deputy Director General. Each deputy meets the Directors and the other officers of the zones in conference and checks on how the Ministry plans are progressing in the districts. The Deputy Directors General regularly meet with the Director General and other senior officers of the Ministry to discuss progress and prepare plans of action.

Performance against the programmed budget is another kind of feedback that the Ministry obtains from the various sub-systems including the Regional Departments of Education. These conferences are held at two levels — at the level of the Ministry, the Deputy Directors General meet with the Director General and his financial advisers, the Chief Accountant and his Accountants and at these conferences the amount and the rate of expenditure are discussed against plans. These conferences also discuss performance in terms of the programmed targets.

Another source of feedback comes from committees and teams visiting schools. The Minister once appointed a high-powered committee, responsible to him, to visit the regions and to sample schools of all types and report to him the schools' progress in respect of all aspects of reforms introduced.

Feedback obtained through the evaluation of student performance gives the Ministry vital information regarding the impact of the total programme at the point that matters most, i.e. at the point of the student. No amount of task-oriented programmes can make up for any lack of impact on the pupil. That is the real test of an objective-oriented management. To obtain this information stratified random samples of pupils who were subjected to the reforms were studied longitudinally in 1972, 1973 and 1974. The data obtained are compared with data obtained in previous years and it is heartening to note that, with the passage of each year, the reforms are taking root. Each sub-system also carries out its own evaluation to check on progress. School inspections carried out by field supervisors also provide the grass-roots data required to improve the quality of instruction. These are conducted throughout the year and are done regionally under the supervision of the Regional Directors of Education and the Chief Education Officers in charge of district. They are also carried out centrally by the Ministry. In fact, the supervision of schools was once the function of a Deputy Director General of Education.

Informal channels

Feedback is also obtained informally from the people, the parents, the students and the politicians. The people, not necessarily the parents, are alive to public issues. Letters to the press and letters to the Ministry are the normal media through which they communicate. Their opinions are respected and, where considered necessary, action is taken on representations made by them.

The parents have a direct interest in education. They not only communicate directly with the officers of the Ministry but also come in deputations to vent their grievances and to have them redressed. Their representations include the lack of teachers, lack of supplies, shortage of accommodation and other matters that affect the education of their children. At times they demand that uncommitted teachers and heads of schools be removed. These representations give the Ministry valuable information on how the reforms are proceeding.

The Ministry has also had dialogue with the students. Students have been invited to the Curriculum Development Centre and their views have been sought not only on how the programmes are functioning, but also on alternative kinds of programmes. These have been some of the most edifying experiences we have so far had.

Politicians are alive to the fact that parents are keenly interested in the education of their children. They, therefore, constitute one of our main sources of information. They represent the people on various statutory and non-statutory bodies and are officially appraised of Ministry programmes. This makes them well informed critics and appraisers.

Communicating

All management processes depend on communication. Control systems, for example, are based almost entirely on systems of communication. The hierarchical structure of the organization regulates information flow. Here we are not concerned with communication theory but with how communication has been harnessed in implementing educational reforms.

Communication also includes diffusion. No reforms in education have any chance of success unless the people themselves are convinced of the need for them. This was realized by the Ministry in 1971 and the most intensive diffusion campaign known in the history of the Ministry was mounted in order to explain the objectives of the reforms and the steps being taken to attain them.

The Secretary and the senior officers of the Ministry visited every region explaining to officers, teachers, parents and the people the thinking behind the changes. Special conferences of all grades of officers were convened at which the reforms were explained and discussed. All available mass media were used in this campaign. There has been no relaxation in this flow of information from the Ministry and in communication with all those concerned.

Within the education system, there is a two-way communication between the upper and lower echelons. The information flow from the top down takes the form of circulars, circular letters, officially sponsored newspapers and face-to-face contact in conferences and meetings. From the lower administration level, there is a regular flow of information to the regional heads of departments and often directly to the Deputy Directors General and the Director General himself.

The Planning Division also functions as a clearing house for information. It conducts the school census once a year, and obtains other vital information in regard to performance against targets. It publishes this information in the form of Ministry handouts. It also maintains a management information system to support vital decision-making. This in brief is how the flow of information and the collection and processing of data takes place in the management of educational reform.

The lateral flow of information is also encouraged. Regional Directors of Education correspond with one another on matters of common interest. In administrative matters such as transfers of teachers, matters of discipline, matters connected with teachers' pensions, Regional Directors transact business directly with one another keeping the Ministry informed, when necessary. In cases of inter-regional transfers where regional balances have to be maintained, the Ministry regulates the procedure. The Deputy Directors General transact business among themselves and often communicate directly with Regional Directors of Education and the Chief Education Officers of districts. In fact this kind of horizontal and sometimes even diagonal communication which takes place regularly in the system, becomes the bulwark on which the Ministry's communication process depends.

5. PHASE OF REPLANNING

It is idle to pretend that such sweeping changes as were introduced in 1972, affecting the systems of primary, junior secondary and senior secondary education and involving about 9,500 schools, 107,000 teachers and approximately 2.5 million pupils, went through just as planned. The feedback indicated a lack of qualified teachers in schools, delays in printing and distributing books and in the supply of equipment. These led to difficulties in implementation which, in turn, necessitated some replanning. At times, even the curriculum, especially in mathematics and science which required specialized staff, had to be modified. Such replanning helped us to achieve increasing success with the passage of each year. In 1972, the year in which the reforms began, many difficulties were encountered. In 1973 the position was better. By 1974 there was confidence that we had weathered the storm. By 1975 we gained enough confidence to go ahead and plan the reforms in the next sector, i.e. in the senior secondary school.

6. RESOURCES

The resources for education — here only the system of formal education is considered — come almost exclusively from the State. The legislation that vested the control and ownership of the assisted schools in the State in 1960 and 1961 did permit a few schools to opt out of the state system. In 1951 too, a few schools opted out of the free education scheme and were allowed to function as private fee-levying schools. But these schools are so few that they do not materially alter the situation of the State being almost the sole financier of education.

The State gets voluntary support from the community to run the school system. This comes by way of donations of permanent or semi-permanent school buildings on a subsidy basis, i.e. the school community subsidizing part of the required expenditure. Schools are also permitted to collect from pupils a fee, termed the services and facilities fee, for services and facilities other than what are normally provided by the schools. This is not a compulsory levy and the amount a school is permitted to collect is very small.

Another source of assistance to education is foreign aid. A team of educational planners who visited Sri Lanka in 1963 in their report[1] had this to say of the foreign aid component:

.....under 4 per cent growth of GNP the estimated internal resources are of the order of Rs. 600/700 million in the year 1981. As against this the estimated foreign aid would be around Rs. 5 million which is less than 1 per cent of the internal resources. A pyramid built on such small additional resources would not alter even the second decimal figure of enrolments which run into millions.

For the fiscal year 1975, the expenditure on formal first and second level education alone is Rs. 659,746,860 and, though no calculation has been made, the foreign aid component today is infinitesimal and may be dismissed as negligible. Of the total estimated expenditure on education for 1975, Rs. 625,857,850 is recurrent expenditure and this is allocated for four programmes as follows:

Programme *Estimate 1975*

1. General administration and staff
   services   30,927,850

---

[1] Unesco Regional Advisory Team for Educational Planning in Asia — *Long Term Projections for Education in Ceylon.* Unesco Regional Office for Education in Asia, Bangkok, 1965.

Programme	Estimate 1975
2. General education	576,952,000
3. Teacher education	10,160,000
4. Technical/vocational education	7,818,000

The largest share by far goes into general education and of this, as in most developing countries, the major share is spent on salaries of teachers.

(For the year 1974 the total recurrent expenditure on education is, according to the Central Bank, 13 per cent of Government's total recurrent expenditure. The total expenditure on education for 1974 is 3.1 per cent of the G. N. P.)

7. CONSTRAINTS INHIBITING PROGRESS

The limiting factors have been mainly resource constraints. Firstly, the new reforms involved the implementation of an enriched curriculum. Whereas a handful of the privileged schools taught science and mathematics under the old order, those subjects were now introduced into the entire school system. This required the supply of science equipment to nearly 6,500 schools. In the recruitment of teachers too there were difficulties. At first, it was the Ministry's intention to recruit as teachers of science and mathematics, the graduates of the 12-year school, i.e. those who had passed at the G.C.E. (Advanced Level) Examination, but there were not enough of them. Therefore, the graduates of the 10-year school, i.e. those who had passed the G.C.E. (Ordinary Level) Examination, had to be recruited. This required redoubling our efforts in in-service education to bring trainees up to scratch as science and mathematics teachers.

The supply of science equipment required foreign exchange and this was hard to get. The Science Curriculum Committee was called upon to prepare a worthwhile scheme that could be taught using available science equipment supplies. Every attempt is being made to design science equipment with available local raw materials and, to this end, a group for the design of such equipment has been set up at the Curriculum Development Centre. When designed, these will be mass produced at the Ministry's Equipment Production Unit.

Lack of resources also plagued as in the matter of printing curriculum guides, textbooks and other background literature. All the curriculum material and the textbooks formerly in use had to be replaced. This required the printing of large numbers of both teacher guides and pupil texts. Paper was in short supply. The few printing presses available were over-loaded with work. The plight we were placed in can well be imagined. The curriculum and textbook committees had to meet deadlines set by the printers which gave them very little time to design, write and try out the material. Printing was often delayed because of equipment breakdown requiring that spare parts be imported from other countries. These were exasperating limitations that had to be endured.

Resource constraint also limited our efforts to establish a dialogue with the people. The available mass media are the newspapers and radio. Newsprint is in short supply and so is radio time. Besides, not every home has a radio receiving set and radio programmes often fail in their impact because very few people listen to them.

We also had to face opposition from unexpected quarters. Far-reaching changes in both the content and structure of education provoked opposition from those who had everything to gain from the old system. The Minister had stated that the reforms are geared to overall development plans and that they had the sanction of the Government. But when fresh representations were made, time and time again, the Ministry officials had to go before the Government to justify their actions — even after the reforms had been launched.

The creation of the Ceylon Education Service did motivate the rank and file of the profession to greater effort. But it too had debilitating effects on the system. Firstly, it caused resentment in the ranks of officers already in the educational administration. The creation of the Ceylon Education Service was bound to affect their promotion prospects and the rights and privileges they enjoyed. Secondly, newcomers into the administration had limited experience in administration. Nevertheless, the service has worked well, and the shortcomings have to be viewed as inevitable in the process of growth toward a better and more representative managerial service.

The trade unions too have been a great strength on the side of the reforming movement. They are new to power and have conducted themselves admirably. Their only shortcoming is that their first concern is to respond to the demands of their members. As trade unions, this is rightly so, but in the future the partnership with the trade unions will be more fruitful as they increase their concern for education.

8. IN RESTROSPECT

Viewing in retrospect the management practices we have used in the implementation of educational reforms, one could discern a mixture of the conventional and unconventional. A perfect system of education management has not yet been evolved, and may never be. Though similarities between a system of education and other systems may be pronounced, dissimilarities also abound. Hence we cannot have recourse to a stereotype. Each country has to draw from its own experience and from the experience of others in formulating its own system of management. A healthy irreverence to all that is conventional is said to be the hallmark of innovative management. Of this, there is plenty of evidence in what has been attempted in Sri Lanka. Not only have the reforms in education been innovative in character, but the management practices that have been used in the implementation of the reforms have been equally innovative. So far, we have not had cause to regret the faith that we placed in our knowledge of things, our long and varied experience and our judgement. Since a perfect system of management of education has not yet been evolved, we will consider any errors of judgement on our part as being inevitable in the process of growth.